The Fairy's Song

A Magical Collection of Fantasy Art, ACEOs, and Rhyme

Cara and Christi Brown

Schiffer Publishing Ltd

4880 Lower Valley Road, Atglen, Pennsylvania 19310

Dedication

This book is dedicated to our wonderful family who encouraged our creativity as children. Mom, Grandma and Grandpa Frederick, Aunt Paula, Kate, Emily, Aunt Linda, Marc, and Soora. Thank you for your continued encouragement and support as well as all the art supplies provided over the years!

Acknowledgments

Text and artwork by Cara and Christi Brown

Title Page: *Child's Play*
ACEO 2008 Cara Brown

Library of Congress Control Number: 2011923215

Designed by Mark David Bowyer
Type set in Zapfino Extra LT Pro / NewBaskerville BT

ISBN: 978-0-7643-3724-6
Printed in China

Schiffer Books are available at special discounts for bulk purchases for sales promotions or premiums. Special editions, including personalized covers, corporate imprints, and excerpts can be created in large quantities for special needs. For more information contact the publisher:

Published by Schiffer Publishing Ltd.
4880 Lower Valley Road
Atglen, PA 19310
Phone: (610) 593-1777; Fax: (610) 593-2002
E-mail: Info@schifferbooks.com

For the largest selection of fine reference books on this and related subjects, please visit our website at
www.schifferbooks.com
We are always looking for people to write books on new and related subjects. If you have an idea for a book please contact us at the above address.

This book may be purchased from the publisher.
Include $5.00 for shipping.
Please try your bookstore first.
You may write for a free catalog.

In Europe, Schiffer books are distributed by
Bushwood Books
6 Marksbury Ave.
Kew Gardens
Surrey TW9 4JF England
Phone: 44 (0) 20 8392-8585; Fax: 44 (0) 20 8392-9876
E-mail: info@bushwoodbooks.co.uk
Website: www.bushwoodbooks.co.uk

Contents

In the Tree Top
ACEO 2006 Christi Brown

Foreword

by Amy Brown

The Fairy's Song is a luminous and enchanting collaboration. Cara and Christi Brown have compiled an eclectic collection of all things fantastical, beautiful, and sometimes a bit dark and mysterious. Cleverly composed poems accompany each image and allow us to see into the hearts of the creatures we've grown up reading about, wondering about, and wishing for. In the true tradition of faeries and other things mysterious and magical, we see that with beauty comes darkness, and within darkness, there is sometimes beauty. Not all things are as they seem. Not only will you catch glimpses of jewel-toned faeries, watery mermaids, and scaled dragons, you will also stumble upon gargoyles, witches, and possibly a pink monkey or two. So follow your heart into the world of "what if." Dance with goblins, dream with dragons, and taste a witch's brew or two. For those of you with wild and magical tastes, *The Fairy's Song* will leave your imagination delightfully full and content.

~Amy Brown, Fairy Artist

About This Book

The Fairy's Song is a collection of original watercolor paintings and poetry created by Cara and Christi Brown between 2005 and 2009. At the end of the book is a gallery of ACEOs or ATCs (art trading cards). ACEO stands for art cards, editions, and originals. They are collectable, original mini-paintings measuring 2 ½" x 3 ½". These tiny paintings are Cara and Christi's favorite outlet of creativity. Hundreds of their original ACEOs have been sold to private collectors all over the world!

"Kawaii" is a word that you will encounter at times in this book. "Kawaii" is a Japanese term for cute, adorable, and sweet. It refers to a unique, cheerful, modern art form originating in Japan that contains simplified rounded shapes, pastel color schemes, and lots of cute smiling faces.

Biography

Growing up in Claremont, California, identical twin sisters Cara and Christi Brown spent most of their childhood creating, drawing and painting together. Their grandfather collected books of artwork by classic artists and the girls were particularly fond of the fantasy themed, colorful, and surreal work of Walt Disney, Salvador Dali, and M.C. Escher. The twins would spend hours examining these wonderful books; and their grandparents, providing them with an endless variety of art supplies, encouraged creativity.

Over the years, Cara and Christi have studied books on various painting and drawing styles and techniques and are largely self-taught. They have come to agree that watercolor is the most versatile and satisfying medium and are enchanted with the unexpected, unique colors and textures that only watercolor can achieve. The twins have also discovered many new artists that provide inspiration including: Daniel Merriam, Arthur Rackham, Brian Froud, David Delamar, Michael Parks, Amy Brown, Jody Bergsma, Mary Englebrite, and Stephanie Pui-Mun Law.

Cara and Christi now reside in the beautiful, peaceful and quiet, beach town of Los Osos, on the central coast of California. They spend the summer months showing and selling their original works and prints at local art fairs and other fantasy themed fairs and festivals. The rest of their free time is spent painting, gardening, and enjoying life. New artwork is regularly posted and can be purchased from their official website CandCFantasyArt.com.

Cara right, Christi left

The Poetry

"Faeries, come take me out of this dull world..."
~William Butler Yeats

Sprites
ACEO 2007 Christi Brown

The Fairy's Song

As it drifts through the woods on a summer's day,
the fairy's song is bright and gay.

Hauntingly lovely like that of a lark,
the fairy's song is soft and dark.

It swirls its way through ferns and leaves,
the fairy's song awakens the trees.

Like delicate bells, notes gently peal.
The fairy's song is magic and real.

All who hear it will frolic and prance,
the fairy's song makes everyone dance.

Like silken fingers caressing your ears,
the fairy's song dissolves all fears.

The music strikes like cupid's dart,
the fairy's song is in your heart.

The Fairy's Ball

The time to celebrate has come,
the midnight hour grows near...
Dressing in their finest gowns
and wearing daisy chains as crowns,
the fairy's ball is here!

All through the night the spirits dance
and sing enchanted song...
Masquerading in delight,
with glow-bug lanterns shinning bright,
they frolic all night long.

Fairy Dreams

Within the Fuchsia Forest of Fae,
where charming pink pixies play pranks all day,
there is one little sprite who is slender and slight,
a dainty, day-dreaming, and darling delight!
The magic around her gleams, glitters, and glows.
The butterflies gather and the gathering grows!
This clever fairy, such a wee little wonder,
has secretly spun the spell you are under!

The Explorer

There one-time was a fairy fine
who built a ship of strange design.
He used some metal scraps and wood
and objects saved since childhood.
A balloon of air to lift it high,
some fairy dust to make it fly!
Propelled by an oar, it seems absurd,
the prow is a mechanical bird!
So up into the sky he went,
to start his fabulous ascent.
Strange new worlds he would explore,
from shining sea to distant shore!

Cara Brown 2005

The Leprechaun

Who is the most famous fairy of all?
Have you ever thought about this?
Is it a large one or is it small,
perhaps we should reminisce...

The noble tooth fairy is one that there is
who is known through all of the land,
'cause money under your pillow she gives
do you think she's the most grand?

Is it the giant that towers above
or is it little Tom Thumb?
There are many more folk I can think of,
pixies and sprites are some...

Is it an elf, a goblin, a troll?
A mermaid, I know it could be...
Is it a hobbit deep in his hole?
That I really can see!

The most very famous fairy of all
is not a brownie or faun;
he actually stands only two feet tall!
And he is the Leprechaun!

Land of Fae

The Land of Fae is a magical place
filled with fanciful features.
Dragons, fairies, elves, and trolls
are some of its many creatures.
There are goblins, sprites,
pixies, and such,
brownies and gnomes
It's just too much!
Mermaids abound
and fauns dance around.
There're nymphs in the trees.
What's that sound on the breeze?
Fairy musicians... the best in the land,
play flutes and drums and in their band,
they've singers and harpists and pipers galore!
You've never heard anything like this before!
Be wary though, if you visit this place
for mischief is mixed with magic and grace.
Beware if you listen when they start to sing
for you can get stuck dancing 'round in a ring!
That's one of the tricks that fairies will play
on those who visit the great Land of Fae!

C. Brown 2008

The Healer

Atop the fairy mountains
and on the highest peak...
just past the sacred grove,
across the crystal creek...

There lives a special fairy
with magic so divine,
that many come to visit
despite the treacherous climb.

This fairy is the healer
of all the Land of Fae.
And if you've any ailments
she'll take them all away!

I See a Fairy!

How do you do? You're a sweet little fairy...
so tiny and precious, jolly and merry!
With thin glossy wings you're as light as a feather,
plum-colored hair and a skin tone like heather!
I really don't know if you' re pixie or sprite
and I see you've a pet. Is he soft? Does he bite?
Although I am tempted to take you back home,
I probably shouldn't. I'll leave you alone.
Delighted and happy I am so very...
It's not every day that you see a fairy!

The Aviator

To pierce the sky and kiss the sun,
there's nothing that compares.
To ride the wind is so much fun...
so free of all your cares.
The pureness of the air, so soft,
caresses as you pass.
The sights you see when you're aloft
can never be surpassed.

To take off in the air and fly
has quite a dangerous feel,
for gravity you dare defy-
that's part of the appeal!
To conquer clouds and part the skies
this is his song and dance.
And so the aviator flies
at every possible chance.

The Dream Seeker

There is a fairy whose job, it seems,
is to seek out all forgotten dreams.
He rides a swan across the sky,
while soft white clouds go billowing by.
Past the sleeping moon he climbs,
a journey he's made a thousand times.

At dusk each night he may be seen
in a velvet suit of aquamarine.
Listen closely, you just might hear...
the jingling bells of his feathered steer.
And when somebody's dreams are lost...
the seeker finds them at any cost!

Playful Mermaid
ACEO 2008 Christi Brown

"...for there is nothing mysterious to a seaman unless it be the sea itself, which is the mistress of his existence and as inscrutable as destiny."

~ Joseph Conrad

The Little Mermaid

Little mermaid of the sea
so very young, wild and free.
A water baby, she's complete,
with scales and fins instead of feet.

A care-free life beneath the green,
cool abyss of the marine—
among the sea reefs and the weeds
where tiny bubbles shine like beads.

But so it goes, like age-old tales,
she's discontent among the whales—
and though her life here seems ideal,
life on land has more appeal.

So she dreams of sunny shore
on which someday she will explore.
If only she could find a way,
there is no price she would not pay.

The only thing to make her whole
requires that she sell her soul.
And if she does indeed transcend
her life at sea will have to end.

Eventually, the tale is told,
to a witch her soul was sold.
Return, she did, to her sea home
to ever drift amongst the foam.

Hidden Beneath

A sea man told me a story one night
of a mermaid 'twas an unnerving sight.
I'll tell you before it gets caught in my throat
the tale he told me, and of him I quote...

"Hidden beneath an odd creature lies,
and if you' re not careful she'll be your demise!"

"She lurks like a serpent casting her charms...
she glides around slowly on octopus arms!

Her lips are so lovely, her skin so fair...
the sound of her voice makes men leap without care!"

"Once in the water you' re stuck in her trap...
around your body her tentacles wrap!
It is told," said the seaman, "once you look in her eyes,
from the depths of the ocean you'll never arise."

"Hidden beneath an odd creature lies,
and if you' re not careful she'll be your demise."

Sea-Dragon Ride

"What joy!"...
the mermaid cried,
"I'm going for a sea-dragon ride!
Such fun...
in store for me,
to ride the shinning scales of he!
Up high...
we'll skim the top
of waves that crash and curl and pop!
Down low...
we'll dive so deep,
we'll twist and turn and splash and leap!
Once done...
we'll count to ten
then we'll do it all again!"

The Pirate Song

Aye Aye...There comes a hearty gale,
the westerly wind, it blasts the sail!
A sailor is one who is stout and true;
together we sail the ocean blue.

Sail pirates sail,
brothers on the sea!
Sail pirates sail...
together we shall be!
Aye, Aye!

Nobel seamen rest assured,
remember to heed the captain's word!
A sailor is one who is brave and strong.
Together we sail till the storm is gone!

Sail pirates sail,
brothers on the sea!
Sail pirates sail...
together we shall be!
Aye, Aye!

The Siren's Song

Come handsome sailors,
come swim with us below.
Listen to our voices,
and feel the water flow.

Come handsome sailors,
leap into sparkling waves,
down in the darkness deep,
down to your watery graves.

Celtic Dolphin

Many a tale has been told
of your magic and grace, since the days of old.
From Irish shores you may be seen
when weather is fair and waters serene.
Far out at sea your fluid shape glides
easily through the waves and the tides.
You carry the hope of luck good and grand
for seafarers both out at sea and on land.
Your subtle smile, intelligent gaze...
swiftness, precision, and playful ways,
has driven you into our history deep
and into our hearts forever you'll keep

E.Brown '06

Admiration

My wonderful friend
you must be in heaven,
such beautiful children you have.
Are there seven?

How lucky you are.
They look just like you!
Even their colors
green-yellow and blue!

Aren't they dainty?
They're so very tiny.
They sparkle like gems.
What makes them so shiny?

And oh, my goodness,
their features are fine!
Such little treasures,
I wish they were mine!

Pygmies

One sort of fairy that I've seldom seen
are the tiny little pygmies of Knollwood Green.
And because these fae are so very small,
I've hardly encountered them ever at all!

If you go into Knollwood Green
take a magnifying glass and eyesight keen.
Early in the morning find a drop of dew,
if the sunlight's good you get just the right view.
You might even see a pygmy seahorse too!

Marjoram
ACEO 2007 Cara Brown

"If you can't take the heat, don't tickle the dragon."

~Unknown Author

Lazy Days

Lazy, dazy, tired, and hazy,
sleeping all day through.
Slow and snoozy, weary, and woozy.
When was the last time you flew?
Nappy, sappy, mindless, and lax
you make other dragons feel shame.
You are just plain lazy and must be crazy,
you've only yourself to blame.

Cara Brown 2007

Moon Dragon

Last night I saw a moon dragon
way up in the sky.
I saw him through the evening mist
upon a cloud so high.
I wanted to talk to the moon dragon
but didn't know how to fly.

I shouted up to the moon dragon
and probably 'woke the town.
In my loudest voice I yelled
"Please sir won't you come down?"
"No way!" yelled the moon dragon
"I don't belong on the ground."

Dragon Dreams

I bet you never thought it true
that dragons dream like me and you.
Their dreams are strange, they change and twist,
but dragon dreams they do exist!
This particular dragon of mine
told me about his dream divine!

My grandmother stood on a cloud by the moon
casting a spell and humming a tune!
I always thought my dreams were bizarre
but my dragon's dreams are better by far!

The Pumpkin Eater

We have got a
Pumpkin Eater!
It's eaten every
single meter
of our cherished
pumpkin patch!
This garden pest
we'll have to catch!

Luckily they're
not that bright
and if we're nice
and real polite,
we'll lure him into
a hot air balloon
and then we'll
send him to the moon!

Hobble the Goblin
ACEO 2008 Christi Brown

"I can bear it no longer! Goblin King! Goblin King! Wherever you may be take this child of mine far away from me!"

~ *The Labyrinth* 1986

cara-Brown 2008

Goblin Hill

There is a place hidden deep...
where the goblin children play
and the goblin children sleep.
A house on the hill built of moss covered stones
has a kitchen well-stocked with bat wings and bones.
The goblin mother is quite a good cook
and makes a fine stew from her recipe book!
And out from the window the mother can see
the frolicking of her dear children three.
They play upon swings and have a fine slide
and on springy animal toys they ride!
When the sun comes up and moonlight dies,
the children return with sleepy eyes!
The house on the hill is now quiet by day,
but at night goblin children will come out to play!

Hobble

Gobble

Sobb

Dobb

The Goblin Brothers

A goblin named Gobble
had a brother named Hobble
and two more brothers had he...
one was named Dobb,
the other named Sobb.
They lived all together you see!

Gobble was a riot,
and Hobble rather quiet.
All were as different could be...
Dobb was quite smart
and Sobb had lost heart,
'cause he longed for a life at sea.

Gobble was a silly guy
Hobble he was rather shy,
some say he was austere...
Dobb was prospective
and Sobb was protective
but they got along fine, I hear.

C. Brown
2008

Almost Midnight

The gargoyle sits upon rooftops high
and waits for midnight to darken the sky.
Far above soot covered chimneys and flues
the sky has lost all of its daytime hues.
When darkness black as ink creeps in
the gargoyle changes his concrete to skin.
And only for one short and fateful hour
the gargoyle can live, breathe, drink and devour!
And visit his brethren on neighboring gable,
or search for a true love, willing and able.
The hour of midnight in London can pass
so swiftly—how gargoyles wish it would last!
Before they know it the time has come,
their bodies will stiffen, grow solid and numb!
For twenty three hours they just have to wait
'til tomorrow night has grown dark and late...

Frog Fairies 2
2007 Christi Brown

"Myths which are believed in tend to become true."

~ George Orwell

Tiger Moth

Tiger Moth upon the wall,
all passers-by she does enthrall.
Kaleidoscope wings that invite attention,
she'll lure you into the other dimension.

The Tiger Moth's fur's colored chalk and coal,
scarlet-red eyes to steal your soul.
Paralyzing all she does confront,
she hath no reason to scavenge or hunt.

The Tiger Moth's goal is to attain
eternal life to continue her reign.
And so she waits, patient and sly,
for an unknowing victim to pass her by.

Owl and Moon

Both owl and moon
are very wise.
One reflects,
the other flies.

The one that flies
needs little light
in the safety
of the night.

The moon will never
get it wrong.
It's been around
so very long.

The owl's great sight
is better when
the moon is out
with glowing grin.

The company they keep
transcends ...
and so the two
remain great friends.

Choche's Dream

In a world full of dreams
he drifts on the breeze.
Is he chasing rabbits
or running from fleas?
An unseen touch twitches his fur
he whimpers and whines,
paws flutter, lips stir.

A thin line divides
what is real and what's not.
Whatever he dreamt
once he wakes he's forgot!

Merlyn's Dream

Merlyn…dreamy mystic being.
What a carefree life you live.
Elegant and grand…
caressing your ghostly face on my hand,
you have so much affection to give.

Oh, to live Merlyn's Dream
in a world free of despair.
You're the Grand Duchess Supreme
with glorious, long, white hair.

Your days are spent being served, like a queen,
whatever it is you demand.
And when you gaze with eyes gold-green
your wish is my command.

Pink Monkeys

Pink monkeys are so special,
pink monkeys are so keen.
They live within the jungle,
so deep and dark and green.
Pink monkeys love the water,
rejoice in getting clean,
and when they're playing in a pond
there's sure to be a scene!

Pink monkeys are so happy,
they love to spend their day,
jumping 'round the waterfall
to pass the time away.
It's very entertaining
to watch them on display,
they splish and splash
and leap and hop,
flip and flop and play!

Pink monkeys like to climb,
on vines they like to swing.
They like to drop from branches high
into the bubbling spring.
Pink monkeys are quite rare,
what joyfulness they bring.
To see them having so much fun
is such a wondrous thing!

The Wizard
ACEO 2008 Christi Brown

"Obsessed by a fairy tale, we spend our lives searching for a magic door and a lost kingdom of peace."

~ Eugene O'Neil

Cara Brown 2008

The Wizard's Apprentice

Once upon a springtime day
I saw some travelers on their way.
One wore feathers white and soft,
the other woven magic cloth.
I listened closely and I heard
that wizard's lecture to the bird.
He said, "Apprentice, listen here
your graduation soon draws near.
You must select a magic wand,
enchanted stick or branch or frond!
Deep in this forest you will find
enchanted plants of many kind.
And only you will know one's right.
Get started! You have until tonight!
And then I'll teach you of its use,"
said this wizard to the goose.
The goose then waddled off the trail.
I wondered if he would prevail.
I never saw the pair again
but think about them now and then.

Immortal Desire

True love burns so deeply
within my breaking heart.
For my love, she's growing old
and from life I will not part.
Alas! She is a mortal
and this torture I must bear,
as I watch while her youth fades
like the color from her hair.
A faun will live forever,
some say "a gift divine,"
but living without love's embrace
will kill this heart of mine.

David Kindlewood and the Magic Owl

David Kindlewood
was sad as could be,
gloomy and glum
and shameful was he!
Because in the wood
he had lost his way,
been thrown off course,
off track, led astray!
His mother had told him
not to go out,
'twas already too dark
and he might lose the route!
And now as the last bit
of daylight dimmed,
the creepy-crawlies
and quivers set in.
Just as David started to cry,
with a "hoot"
a magical owl flew by.
He dried his eyes
and himself pulled together,
cause in the owl's tail
gleamed a bright glowing feather!
He ran after that bird,
its light source he needed,
he chased and he paced
and then finally succeeded!
Astonished was he
when he looked around.
He could not believe
he was home safe and sound!
David was embarrassed,
his mother was mad,
but David, he knew
a good lesson'd been had!
Listen to your mother
when she says what to do,
it isn't very often
that magic will save you!

Landrina and the Unicorn

Landrina was a princess who
lived in the days of olde,
and legend has it that she saved
the last unicorn, we're told.

In the woods she encountered one night
a mystical, magical steed,
whose spellbinding horn, so silver and bright
was the tool of her own father's greed.

Her father had captured this last unicorn,
it's one single gem to attain.
For if one was able to dis-adorn,
eternal youth he would gain!

So Landrina poured a strong sleeping potion
into the household's wine,
and escaped with the beast, with true devotion,
just in the last nick of time.

And to this day the king does mourn
the loss of his dear little princess,
who fearlessly rescued the last unicorn
whose legend will always be ageless.

The Minstrel's Song

Play some merry music please,
oh minstrel, while I dine!
Songs of love and distant seas,
while I sip my scarlet wine.

Sing to me with cheerful heart,
play for me a jolly tune.
Tales superb, please, do impart,
on this lonely afternoon.

For my heart... it's in a dither.
I know you can make it warm.
So, please minstrel, do come hither
and for me please do perform!

Play some merry music, do!
And if you've got the time
speak to me of love so true
in song and dance and rhyme!

Kawaii World

Cotton candy clouds and infinite sun,
Kawaii World is so fun, fun, fun!
Pastel rainbows and smiling fruit,
nothing on Earth is so cute, cute, cute!
Take a look around, everything's a treat!
Everything you see looks so sweet, sweet, sweet!
Whatever it may be, it's pretty and dear;
Kawaii World makes us cheer, cheer, cheer!

2007
Cara Braun

Hansel and Gretel

Stretched taffy trees,
a black liquorice road,
unbridled dreams
served a la mode...

Gum drops and candy canes,
sweet chocolate bliss,
no child could resist
allure quite like this.

But into open jaws...
little feet might tread,
mouths filled with candy corn,
mint and gingerbread.

Beware of quaint illusions,
for tempting they may be...
We all know that evil lurks
near candied rocks and trees...

Cara Brown

Alice in Wonderland

Some dreams are big and some are quite small.
Alice dreamed the most grand dream of all.
Innermost thoughts subliminally cast,
thoughts from today, from the future, and past.
Woven together a great tale was spun
that lives in our hearts and will not be outdone.

Wonderland dreams afloat on the breeze,
magical mushrooms and tear-filled seas.
Up in a tree a Cheshire Cat grins
and the hatter's as mad as the
strange Tweedle twins!

Some stories linger and endear us so long,
ingrained in our minds like a poem or a song.
We let go of our worries and reach for her hand,
and go back with Alice to Wonderland.

Fall
Cara Brown, 2005

The Green Man

Claim your siege aright you should,
Green Man of the wild wood.

Green Man, spirit of the trees,
Green Man, with your face of leaves.

Reflection of a long time gone,
into our open hearts be drawn.
To your song plagued souls shall drum,
your renaissance ere long shall come.

Green Man bring hope for our earth,
Green Man symbol of rebirth.

Father nature's time is nigh,
Green Man will you hear our cry?
Green Man loyal Goddess lover,
old faith in our hearts uncover.

Bring us hope for Mother Earth,
Green Man symbol of rebirth.
Green Man God of shelter and shade,
your legend nary ever will fade.

Claim your siege aright you should,
Green Man of the wild wood.

Ivy
ACEO 2006 Christi Brown

"On Halloween, witches come true; Wild ghosts escape from dreams. Each monster dances in the park...."

~ Nicholas Gordon

C. Brown '06

Gathering With the Crows

Such a magical time of year
when summer is gone and autumn is here.
The days grow shorter, the sky's getting grey,
the wind swirls around making tree branches sway.
The magic that rides on the wind is complete.
Nature's a fabulous, bountiful treat!
Red pomegranates glisten like jewels,
from fallen leaves grow new toad-stools!
The ravens and crows like to frolic and chatter,
they play their games making dead leaves scatter.
This is the time of year for the witches
to gather the finest of nature's sweet riches.
To use in their potions, elixirs, and brews,
to heal, bring true love, or to simply amuse.
At the end of the month is the most special day,
when the dead come to visit, to haunt, and to play.
There's no other time in the year quite as keen
or as hauntingly magic as Halloween!

Queen of Frogs

Rarely in summer a rain cloud appears
bringing with it saltless tears.

It happens once in a blue moon,
when all is dried up like a prune.

And with it comes the Queen of Frogs
with all her grown-up pollywogs!

When rain drops hit the hot, dry earth
this summons the frogs to their re-birth!

"Come one, come all, come join your queen.
Rise from the earth, so moist and green.
Come forth my frogs, this rain won' t last
for in a blink it will have passed!
And soon the clouds will stop their cry,
the earth again will start to dry!"

The Queen of Frogs must now retreat
and quickly gather up her fleet.

Go back into the cool wet mud,
dormant till the next rain's flood.

Go back Queen of Frogs until the Fall,
Go back Queen of Frogs, take one, take all!

The Halloween Tree

On the eve of Hallow's night,
with jack-o-lanterns glowing bright,
up in the branches of a tree,
the night is bathed in ghostly glee.

Pumpkins placed with utmost care
light up the cool, crisp swirling air.
Faces carved to ward the dead,
look like the horse-man's long lost head!

Deep in the woods among the trees,
the very sight will shake your knees.
An eerie scene you can' t deny,
enough to make small children cry.

The beacon is a meeting site
for haunting partners to unite.
When the witching hour's done
or before it has begun.

The tree is where the witches meet
when Hallow's haunting is complete.
A place to boast about the fright
created on this Hallow's night!

The Magic Forest
ACEO 2009 Cara Brown

Happy Mushrooms
ACEO 2009 Christi Brown

Fairy and Peacock
ACEO 2006 Christi Brown

Spriteling
ACEO 2009 Christi Brown

The ACEO Gallery:

Fairies

Fairy Maiden
ACEO 2009 Christi Brown

My Pet Dragon
ACEO 2009 Cara Brown

The Good Fairy
ACEO 2008 Cara Brown

The Explorer
ACEO 2009 Christi Brown

Blackwings
ACEO 2008 Christi Brown

Mushroom Cap
ACEO 2008 Christi Brown

Bee My Friend
ACEO 2008 Christi Brown

Elfin Fairy
ACEO 2009 Christi Brown

Kalina
ACEO 2009 Christi Brown

Flower Fairy
ACEO 2009 Cara Brown

Little Pixie Fairy
ACEO 2009 Christi Brown

Moonlight
ACEO 2008 Cara Brown

Mushroom Fairy
ACEO 2008 Cara Brown

Brownie
ACEO 2009 Christi Brown

Best Friends
ACEO 2008 Cara Brown

The Aviator
ACEO 2008 Christi Brown

Old Friends
ACEO 2008 Christi Brown

Fairy's Ball 1
ACEO 2008 Christi Brown

Fairy's Ball 2
ACEO 2008 Christi Brown

Autumn Fire Fairy
ACEO 2008 Christi Brown

Little Secret
ACEO 2007 Christi Brown

Carrot Raider
ACEO 2008 Christi Brown

Radish Raider
ACEO 2007 Christi Brown

Winter Fairy
ACEO 2008 Cara Brown

Shy Violet
ACEO 2008 Christi Brown

Fae of the Dragon
ACEO 2008 Christi Brown

Woodland Fairy
ACEO 2008 Christi Brown

Snow Fairy
ACEO 2008 Christi Brown

Tribal Fairy
ACEO 2007 Cara Brown

Goth Fairy
ACEO 2007 Christi Brown

Snail and Fairy
ACEO 2006 Christi Brown

Surprise
ACEO 2006 Christi Brown

Autumn Fairy
ACEO 2006 Christi Brown

Jella
ACEO 2006 Christi Brown

Rainbow Sprite
ACEO 2006 Christi Brown

Pumpkin Fairy
ACEO 2006 Christi Brown

The Sea Shore
ACEO 2008 Christi Brown

Shipwrecked
ACEO 2008 Christi Brown

Mermaid Bay
ACEO 2007 Christi Brown

Eyes of Gold
ACEO 2007 Cara Brown

Mermaids

Fishing
ACEO 2008 Cara Brown

Mermaid Motif
ACEO 2008 Christi Brown

Yellow Skies
3.75in x 2.5in 2008
Christi Brown

An Offering
ACEO 2008 Christi Brown

Anglerfish
2009 Cara Brown

Kawaii Mermaid
ACEO 2008 Christi Brown

Merbaby
ACEO 2008 Cara Brown

Bubbles
ACEO 2007
Christi Brown

Seadragon Gargoyle
ACEO 2008 Cara Brown

Mrs. Seaworthy
ACEO 2009 Christi Brown

Mr. Seaworthy
ACEO 2008 Christi Brown

Elora
ACEO 2008 Christi Brown

Little Sea Dragon
ACEO 2008
Christi Brown

Mr. Seaward
ACEO 2007 Christi Brown

Sea Dragon
ACEO 2008 Christi Brown

Blue Heron
ACEO 2009 Cara Brown

Egret
ACEO 2009 Cara Brown

Siren
ACEO 2008 Christi Brown

The Dragon and the Rose
ACEO 2007 Christi Brown

The Rose and the Dragon
ACEO 2007 Christi Brown

Sunset Dragon
ACEO 2008 Cara Brown

Copper
ACEO 2008 Christi Brown

Dragons

Amulet
ACEO 2008 Cara Brown

Dragon City
ACEO 2009 Christi Brown

Golden Dragon
ACEO 2008 Cara Brown

Blue Dragon
ACEO 2008 Christi Brown

The Protector
ACEO 2008 Cara Brown

Dragon Kisses
ACEO 2006 Christi Brown

The Dragon
ACEO 2007 Christi Brown

Sorcery
ACEO 2006 Christi Brown

Discussing Magic
ACEO 2006 Christi Brown

New Addition
ACEO 2008 Christi Brown

Dragon Eggs
ACEO 2006 Christi Brown

Dragon Moon
ACEO 2007 Cara Brown

Luck Dragon
ACEO 2008 Cara Brown

Patience
ACEO 2009 Christi Brown

A Moment in Time
ACEO 2008 Christi Brown

The Goblin King
ACEO 2009 Christi Brown

The Hob Goblin
ACEO 2008 Christi Brown

Goblins, Gargoyles, and Monsters

Fuzzy Wuzzy
ACEO 2008 Cara Brown

Goblin Hill
ACEO 2008 Cara Brown

Goblin Land
ACEO 2008 Cara Brown

Little Monster
ACEO 2007 Christi Brown

The Crystal Hat
ACEO 2008 Cara Brown

Gobble the Goblin
ACEO 2008 Christi Brown

Dobb the Goblin
ACEO 2008 Christi Brown

Sobb the Goblin
2008 Christi Brown

Clobb the Goblin
ACEO 2008 Christi Brown

Baby Goblin
ACEO 2008 Cara Brown

Pondering
ACEO 2008 Christi Brown

Waiting
ACEO 2009 Christi Brown

Gargoyle Fairy
ACEO 2007 Christi Brown

Goblin and Snail
ACEO 2009 Christi Brown

Ready or Not
ACEO 2008 Cara Brown

Hide and Seek
ACEO 2008 Cara Brown

Little Gremlin
ACEO 2006 Cara Brown

Bobble the Goblin
ACEO 2008 Christi Brown

Winged Black Cat 2
ACEO 2008 Cara Brown

Cloud Cruiser
ACEO 2008 Cara Brown

Fox Fairy
ACEO 2008 Christi Brown

Carousel Ostrich
ACEO 2008 Cara Brown

Magical Animals

Hummingbird
ACEO 2009 Christi Brown

Moonlight Romance
ACEO 2009 Christi Brown

Lunch Time
ACEO 2009 Christi Brown

Bear Bay
ACEO 2009 Cara Brown

Winged Brown Cat
ACEO 2008 Christi Brown

Fairy Kittens
ACEO 2009 Christi Brown

Curious Butterfly
ACEO 2009 Christi Brown

Midnight Garden
ACEO 2009 Cara Brown

Proud Catch
ACEO 2006 Christi Brown

Otherworld Owls
ACEO 2009 Cara Brown

Winged Calico 1
ACEO 2008 Cara Brown

Winged Calico 3
ACEO 2008 Cara Brown

Winged Calico 2
ACEO 2008 Cara Brown

Winged Black Cat 1
ACEO 2008 Cara Brown

Mountain Goat
ACEO 2009 Christi Brown

Hummingbird 2
ACEO 2009 Christi Brown

Spring Chickens
ACEO 2009 Cara Brown

Little Fawn
ACEO 2009 Christi Brown

Kawaii Fawn
ACEO 2009 Christi Brown

Hummingbird and Cat Tails
ACEO 2008 Christi Brown

Worried
ACEO 2008 Christi Brown

Shelly the Snail
ACEO 2008 Christi Brown

Whimsical
ACEO 2009 Christi Brown

Puppy Fairy
ACEO 2008 Cara Brown

Lost at Sea
ACEO 2008 Cara Brown

Luna
ACEO 2008 Cara Brown

Owls and Roses
ACEO 2008 Cara Brown

Captain Smokey
ACEO 2008 Cara Brown

Baby Bunny
ACEO 2008 Cara Brown

Flying High
ACEO 2008 Cara Brown

Wise Old Owl
ACEO 2007 Cara Brown

Two Moon Owls
ACEO 2007 Cara Brown

Buzzard
ACEO 2008 Christi Brown

The Watcher
ACEO 2006 Christi Brown

Under the Oak
ACEO 2008 Cara Brown

Crystal Worm
ACEO 2008 Cara Brown

The Underworld
ACEO 2007 Cara Brown

Jester Monkey
ACEO 2007 Christi Brown

The Retriever
ACEO 2008 Cara Brown

Rainbow Frog
ACEO 2007 Cara Brown

Fox Cub
ACEO 2009 Cara Brown

Fox Cubs
ACEO 2009 Christi Brown

Red Fox
ACEO 2009 Cara Brown

Eclipse
ACEO 2007 Cara Brown

Windsong
ACEO 2009 Christi Brown

The Green Man
ACEO 2008 Christi Brown

Merlin
ACEO 2007 Christi & Cara Brown

Red Riding Hood
ACEO 2007 Cara Brown

Fairy Tales and Mythical Creatures

Door Mouse
ACEO 2009 Christi Brown

Dum and Dee
ACEO 2008 Cara Brown

Cheshire Cat
ACEO 2008 Christi Brown

Young Queen of Hearts
ACEO 2008 Christi Brown

Dee and Dum
ACEO 2008 Cara Brown

Rapunzel
ACEO 2007 Cara Brown

Kawaii Faun
ACEO 2009 Christi Brown

Little Faun
ACEO 2008 Christi Brown

Little Miss Muffet
ACEO 2007 Christi Brown

Pan
ACEO 2007 Cara Brown

Peter Pumpkin Eater
ACEO 2007 Christi Brown

Jack in the Green
ACEO 2007 Christi Brown

The Warrior
ACEO 2008 Christi Brown

Drink Me
ACEO 2008 Christi Brown

Queen of Hearts Card
ACEO 2007 Cara Brown

Mad Hatter
ACEO 2008 Christi Brown

Queen of Hearts
ACEO 2008 Christi Brown

Pink Cheshire Cat
ACEO 2007 Cara Brown

Pool of Tears
ACEO 2007 Cara Brown

The Mad Tea Party
ACEO 2007 Cara Brown

The White Rabbit
ACEO 2007 Cara Brown

Alice and the Cheshire Cat
ACEO 2007 Cara Brown

Alice in a Bottle
ACEO 2008 Christi Brown

Cheshire Cat 2
ACEO 2008 Cara Brown

Crying Alice
ACEO 2007 Cara Brown

Humpty Dumpty
ACEO 2007 Christi Brown

The Caterpillar
ACEO 2008 Christi Brown

Alice and the White Rabbit
ACEO 2007 Cara Brown

5 of Hearts
ACEO 2008 Christi Brown

Purple Caterpillar
ACEO 2009 Christi Brown

Red Rose
ACEO 2008 Cara Brown

Little Wizard 2
ACEO 2007 Christi Brown

Little Gnome
ACEO 2008 Cara Brown

Little Wizard
ACEO 2007 Christi Brown

Gathering Violets
ACEO 2008 Cara Brown

Garden Gnome
ACEO 2006 Christi Brown

Petunia
ACEO 2008 Cara Brown

Leprechaun
ACEO 2007 Cara Brown

Leprechaun 2
ACEO 2007 Cara Brown

The Magician
ACEO 2008 Cara Brown

The Elfin Guard
ACEO 2007 Christi Brown

The Elfin Drummer
ACEO 2006 Christi Brown

Wendy
ACEO 2008 Christi Brown

Pumpkin Spice
ACEO 2009 Christi Brown

Estella
ACEO 2007 Christi Brown

Ostara
ACEO 2007 Cara Brown

Mandy and Randy
ACEO 2008 Christi Brown

The Blues
ACEO 2008 Christi Brown

Rowanna
ACEO 2008 Christi Brown

Alexandra
ACEO 2007 Christi Brown

Little Apple Pie
ACEO 2007 Christi Brown

Learning the Basics
ACEO 2007 Christi Brown

Weird Wendy
ACEO 2007 Christi Brown

Cassandra
ACEO 2007 Christi Brown

Enchanted
ACEO 2007 Christi Brown

Prize Pumpkin
ACEO 2007 Christi Brown

Haunting Time
ACEO 2009 Cara Brown

Periwinkle Pumpkins
ACEO 2007 Christi Brown

Witch's Brew
ACEO 2007 Christi Brown

Mary Anne
ACEO 2007 Cara Brown

Calling the Wind
ACEO 2007 Cara Brown

Storybook Witch
ACEO 2007 Christi Brown

Bookhouse Witch
ACEO 2007 Christi Brown

Stella Sandershans
ACEO 2007 Christi Brown

Stella Sandershans 2
ACEO 2007 Christi Brown

Stella Sandershans 3
ACEO 2007 Christi Brown

Brown Eyed Susan
ACEO 2007 Christi Brown

Pollyanna
ACEO 2007 Christi Brown

Winifred Winkle 2
ACEO 2006 Christi Brown

Saved by the Spell
ACEO 2006 Christi Brown

Winifred Winkle
ACEO 2006 Christi Brown

Wanda Winkle
ACEO 2007 Christi Brown

Abigail
ACEO 2007 Christi Brown

Anastasia
ACEO 2007 Christi Brown

Storm Crows
ACEO 2006 Christi Brown

Foxy Witch
ACEO 2006 Christi Brown

Desolate
ACEO 2007 Christi Brown

Bonnie Broom
ACEO 2006 Christi Brown

Witch Two Owls
ACEO 2006 Christi Brown

Trick or Treat?
ACEO 2006 Christi Brown

Star
ACEO 2006
Christi Brown

White Jack
ACEO 2006 Cara Brown

White Jack Stack
ACEO 2006 Cara Brown

Moon Wish
ACEO 2006 Cara Brown

Little Trick or Treater
ACEO 2006 Cara Brown

Blue Baby Lewis
ACEO 2006 Christi Brown

Pomegranate 2
ACEO 2006 Christi Brown

Pomegranate
ACEO 2006 Christi Brown

Delilah
ACEO 2006 Christi Brown

Delilah 2
ACEO 2006 Christi Brown

Glenda Grapes 2
ACEO 2006 Christi Brown

Glenda Grapes
ACEO 2006 Christi Brown

Prickly Pears
ACEO 2006 Christi Brown

Baby Lewis
ACEO 2008 Christi Brown

Prickly Pears 2
ACEO 2006 Christi Brown

Pumpkin
ACEO 2006 Christi Brown

Pumpkin 2
ACEO 2006 Christi Brown

Cherrie
ACEO 2006 Christi Brown

Pumpkin Brown 2
ACEO 2006 Christi Brown

Pumpkin Brown 3
ACEO 2007 Christi Brown

Pumpkin and Baby Lewis
ACEO 2006 Christi Brown

Pumpkin Brown
ACEO 2006 Christi Brown

My Pet Frog
ACEO 2006 Christi Brown

Kawaii Island
ACEO 2009 Cara Brown

Pear Tree
ACEO 2009 Cara Brown

Rubber Duckies
ACEO 2008 Cara Brown

Monkey Suit
ACEO 2009 Cara Brown

More ACEOs

The Magic Blanket 2
ACEO 2009 Cara Brown

The Magic Blanket 3
ACEO 2009 Cara Brown

Little Princess
ACEO 2009 Cara Brown

The Magic Blanket 1
ACEO 2009 Cara Brown

Sunflower Light
ACEO 2006 Cara Brown

Kawaii in the Sky
ACEO 2009 Cara Brown

The Jumper
ACEO 2007 Cara Brown

The Dreamer
ACEO 2007 Cara Brown

Candy Land
ACEO 2009 Cara Brown

Butterfly Bug
ACEO 2007
Christi Brown

Kawaii in the Sky 2
ACEO 2009 Cara Brown

Little Angel
ACEO 2009 Cara Brown

Bath Time
ACEO 2009 Cara Brown

Too Much Fun
ACEO 2009 Cara Brown

Martians on Wheels
ACEO 2009 Cara Brown

Peacock Suit
ACEO 2007 Cara Brown

Up and Away
ACEO 2009 Christi Brown

Little Hula Hooper
ACEO 2009 Cara Brown